WHEN I GROW UP
I'LL BE A DOCTOR

BY CONNIE COLWELL MILLER   ILLUSTRATED BY SILVIA BARONCELLI

AMICUS ILLUSTRATED · RIVERSTREAM

AMICUS ILLUSTRATED is published by Amicus
P.O. Box 1329, Mankato, MN 56002
www.amicuspublishing.us

Paperback edition printed by RiverStream Publishing in arrangement with Amicus.
ISBN 978-1-62243-361-2 (paperback)

LIBRARY OF CONGRESS CATALOGING-IN-PUBLICATION DATA
Names: Miller, Connie Colwell, 1976- author. | Baroncelli, Silvia, illustrator.
Title: I'll be a doctor / by Connie Colwell Miller ; illustrated by Silvia Baroncelli.
Other titles: I will be a doctor
Description: Mankato, MN : Amicus, [2016] | Series: When I grow up . . . |
  Series: Amicus illustrated | Audience: K to grade 3.
Identifiers: LCCN 2015029345 | ISBN 9781607537601 (library binding) |
ISBN 9781607538592 (ebook)
Subjects: LCSH: Physicians–Juvenile literature.
Classification: LCC R707 .M57 2016 | DDC 610.69/5—dc23
LC record available at http://lccn.loc.gov/2015029345

EDITOR   Rebecca Glaser
DESIGNER   Kathleen Petelinsek

Printed in the United States of America at
Corporate Graphics in North Mankato, Minnesota.

HC 10 9 8 7 6 5 4 3 2 1
PB 10 9 8 7 6 5 4 3 2 1

ABOUT THE AUTHOR

Connie Colwell Miller is a writer, reader, and teacher who lives in Mankato, Minnesota. When she was little she always knew she would work with two things: kids and books. Today, her dream has come true. She has written more than 80 books for kids, and she has four wonderful, creative children of her own.

ABOUT THE ILLUSTRATOR

Silvia Baroncelli has loved to draw since she was a child. She collaborates regularly with publishers in drawing and graphic design from her home in Prato, Italy. Her best collaborators are her four nephews, daughters Ginevra and Irene, and organized husband Tommaso. Find out more about her at silviabaroncelli.it

Today my little b... .... is going to the doctor for a checkup. Every time I go to Dr. Davis's office, I pretend ...

… I'm the pediatrician, Dr. Amy Bell! All my patients are babies and kids. I'm like a superhero who helps sick kids feel better and keeps healthy kids healthy.

My first patient needs a checkup. I listen to his lungs and heart with my stethoscope. I look in his eyes, ears, and throat with my otoscope. I check his reflexes.

I ask about the boy's food, sleep, and activities. When everything checks out, I smile and say to him, "You're healthy as an ox!" This is what Dr. Davis always says to me.

My next patient has a sore throat. I use a tongue depressor and the otoscope again. This time, I see red! This little guy needs medicine to help him feel better.

His dad is worried. But I know just the medicine this little guy needs. I write a prescription. The special little guy will be feeling better soon.

We track our patients' medicines and health problems on the computer. Then we can check the records when the patient comes in again.

So I ask for help from other doctors. I send this girl to the cardiologist, Dr. Hill. He is an expert on people's hearts. He will know what to do to make her feel better.

When I grow up, I'll be a real doctor. But now, Dr. Davis is here to see my brother Malcolm. She'll make sure he's healthy as an ox … so he can play doctor with me all afternoon!

cardiologist—A doctor who works on people's hearts.

otoscope—A tool with a light used for looking inside the eyes, ears, and throat.

pediatrician—A doctor who works with babies and children.

prescription—A note written by a doctor that allows you to buy medicine.

stethoscope—A tool that allows doctors to hear your lungs and heart.

vaccination—A shot of medicine that helps prevent disease.

Ask an adult to help you put together a real first-aid kit.
You can help if someone in your family gets hurt.

WHAT YOU NEED

- ☐ 25 adhesive bandages, different sizes
- ☐ antibiotic ointment
- ☐ antiseptic wipes
- ☐ hydrocortisone ointment
- ☐ 1 roller bandage
- ☐ oral thermometer
- ☐ tweezers
- ☐ cotton balls or swabs
- ☐ hydrogen peroxide
- ☐ first-aid instruction booklet

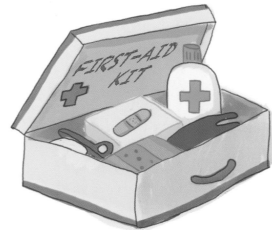

WHAT YOU DO

Place all your first-aid items in a small box or bag. Keep the bag in a safe and easy-to-reach place. If someone gets hurt, ask an adult for help.